How to Draw the Life and Times of
Franklin Pierce

Dulce Zamora

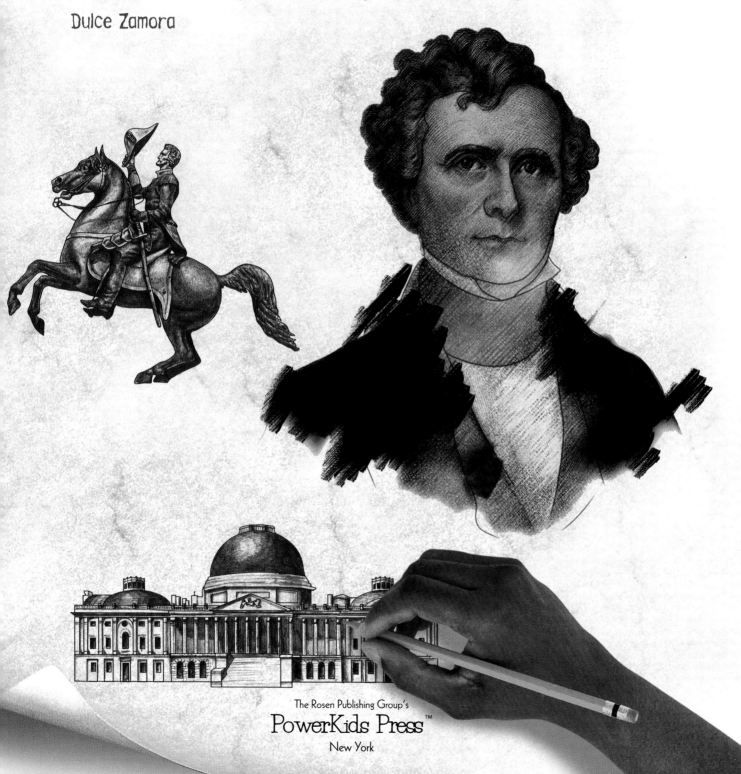

The Rosen Publishing Group's
PowerKids Press™
New York

To my dear Noely,
You are my sunshine and my rock.
Thank you

Published in 2006 by The Rosen Publishing Group, Inc.
29 East 21st Street, New York, NY 10010

First Edition

Editor: Rachel O'Connor
Layout Design: Elana Davidian

Illustrations: All illustrations by Michelle Innes.
Photo Credits: pp. 4, 10, 20 (left) © Bettman/Corbis; p. 7 White House Historical Association (White House Collection 14); p. 8 Picture History; pp. 9, 12, 26, © North Wind Picture Archives; p. 14 © Robert Holmes/Corbis; pp. 16, 18 (left) © Library of Congress Prints and Photographs Division; pp. 18 (right), 24 © Corbis; p. 20 (right) © MAPS.com/Corbis; p. 22 Courtesy of The New Hampshire Historical Society; p. 28 © Getty Images.

Library of Congress Cataloging-in-Publication Data

Zamora, Dulce.
How to draw the life and times of Franklin Pierce / Dulce Zamora.— 1st ed.
    p. cm. — (A kid's guide to drawing the presidents of the United States of America)
Includes bibliographical references and index.
ISBN 1-4042-2991-4 (lib. bdg.)
1. Pierce, Franklin, 1804–1869—Juvenile literature. 2. Presidents—United States—Biography—Juvenile literature. 3. Drawing—Technique—Juvenile literature. I. Title. II. Series.

E432.Z36 2006
973.6'6'092—dc22

                    2004021628

Manufactured in the United States of America

Contents

True Follower of the Constitution

President Franklin Pierce led the United States from 1853 to 1857, in a period of promise and conflict. It was a time of hope because new states were joining the Union and opening up their land to settlers. The question of whether the new territories would be slave or free,  however, was an ongoing problem. Pierce tried to avoid the issue. He believed the Constitution gave the federal government little authority to make such choices, and that it was a matter for the states to decide. This view made him unpopular with the northern states, who were against slavery. Even so he continued to follow the law.

Franklin Pierce was born on November 23, 1804, in a log cabin in Hillsborough, New Hampshire. He was the sixth of eight children raised by General Benjamin Pierce and Anna Kendrick. His father fought in the American Revolution and served twice as governor of New Hampshire. As a young boy,

Franklin wanted to prove himself on the battlefield as his father had, but General Pierce wanted his son to finish school. The general wanted Franklin to have the college education he never had.

After studying law for three years, Pierce became a lawyer in 1827. He soon followed his father into politics. Beginning in 1829, he served as a representative to the New Hampshire legislature. In 1833, he became a U.S. congressman and in 1837, he became a senator. He left political life in 1842 to improve his finances by going back into law and to spend more time with his wife and children.

You will need the following supplies to draw the life and times of Franklin Pierce:

✓ A sketch pad   ✓ An eraser   ✓ A pencil   ✓ A ruler

These are some of the shapes and drawing terms you need to know:

Horizontal Line	—	Squiggly Line	∿
Oval	⬭	Trapezoid	⏢
Rectangle	▭	Triangle	△
Shading	▰	Vertical Line	|
Slanted Line	/	Wavy Line	∿

The Fourteenth President of the United States

Franklin Pierce's dream to become a soldier like his father came true in 1846, when the United States declared, or announced, war on Mexico. He was appointed as brigadier general of a volunteer group of men. Although injuries kept him mostly off the battlefield, Pierce did his best to serve his country.

Pierce soon had another chance to serve the Union. In 1852, he was elected president of the United States.

Pierce worked hard to lead a country divided by the issue of slavery. In 1854, he signed the Kansas-Nebraska Act into law. The act gave the two new territories the right to vote on whether they wanted to be free or slave states. Pierce hoped that this freedom of choice would help settle arguments. It did not. Fighting in Kansas broke out in May 1856, destroying Pierce's hopes of a presidential nomination the following month. He did not get reelected and on March 3, 1857, he left the White House an unpopular president.

Pierce became the U.S. president on March 4, 1853. His term, however, began in sorrow. His 11-year-old son had died in a train accident in January of that year. Also, shortly after his term started, his vice president, William R. King, died from an illness.

Franklin Pierce's New Hampshire

Such well-known people as Daniel Webster and Nathaniel Hawthorne came to visit the tavern in Pierce's childhood home.

New Hampshire

Map of the United States of America

Many of the places important to the fourteenth president of the United States can be found near New Hampshire's Route 9, which is also known as the Franklin Pierce Highway. The highway passes by Hillsborough, where Pierce was born and raised. His childhood home is now a museum. Inside the house visitors can see the tavern the family opened up for extra income during Franklin's childhood. At the time the tavern was a popular stop for people going to the state capital of Concord.

On Main Street in Concord, also off Route 9, is the State House, where Franklin Pierce worked as a representative in the state legislature from 1829 to 1833. Tours of the State House are available. In front of the building is a bronze statue of Pierce, which was erected in 1914. It is the only statue of the past president in his home state.

Concord became Pierce's home in 1838. He moved there with his wife, Jane, and opened up a law office. The house where they lived, called the Pierce Manse, is now open to the public. On display is a picture of the couple's son Frank Robert, who died of typhoid fever in 1843, at the age of four.

The governor of New Hampshire, Samuel D. Felker, gave a speech on November 25, 1914, to mark the completion of the Franklin Pierce statue in front of Concord's State House. In his speech Felker repeated something Senator Bainbridge Wadleigh had said, "But for slavery, and the questions growing out of it, [Franklin Pierce's] administration would have passed into history as one of the most successful in our national life."

His Father's Son

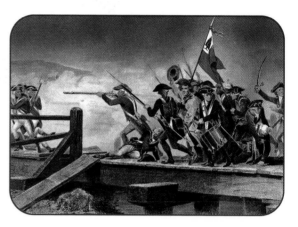

As a boy Franklin Pierce looked up to his father. Benjamin Pierce was a hero of the American Revolution. In 1775, Benjamin was working on his uncle's field when he first learned that fighting with the British had begun in Lexington, Massachusetts. Benjamin immediately grabbed his gun and powder horn and joined the war. He served in the Continental army for nine years. George Washington honored him as a valuable officer.

After the war Benjamin settled on a farm in New Hampshire. It was here that his wife, Anna Kendrick gave birth to Franklin and seven other children. Their home was sometimes open as a tavern for travelers along the highway. Young Franklin would often hear his father share war stories and talk about politics with guests. Franklin dreamt of fighting in battles like the one pictured here, in Concord, where some of the first shots of the American Revolution were fired.

1

To begin the drummer from the Battle of Concord, draw a vertical line. Draw an oval as a guide for the head, and a rectangle as a guide for the body.

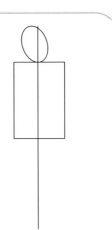

2

Draw a slanted line coming from the bottom of the rectangle where it meets the vertical line. Draw four flat ovals as guides for the drummer's calves and feet.

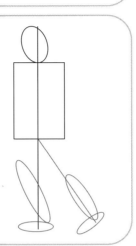

3

Draw lines as shown for the drummer's shoulders, body, arms, and hands using the rectangular guide. Add another rectangle, with a curved top and bottom, for the drum.

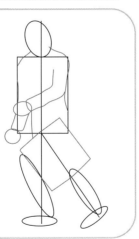

4

Draw a slanted line across the face. Draw the outline for the hat, hair, and chin. Add lines for his fists and fingers. Draw his legs and feet. Add a curvy line for the tail of the jacket.

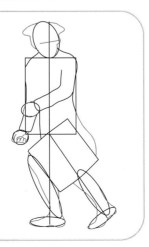

5

Erase all guides except the oval head guide. Add details to the hat as shown. Draw lines down the front of the body for the drum straps. Draw drumsticks and add details to the drum.

6

Add more lines for drum straps. Draw lines for the sword as shown. Draw the curved shapes for the sword handle. Add the curvy lines around the body for the strap that holds the sword.

7

Finish the face by drawing the eyes, nose, and mouth. Add lines for the side of the head and for the ear. Erase any extra lines. Add details to the collar of the jacket and the shoes as shown.

8

Erase the eye guide. Finish the drawing by shading in as much as you can. Notice where the shading is darker in some areas. Well done. You have finished.

Student Life

In 1812, the United States began fighting the War of 1812 with Britain. Eight-year-old Franklin wanted to join the battles, as his brothers had done, but his parents sent him 2 miles (3.2 km) away to the little brick schoolhouse in Hillsborough Center instead. When he was 12 years old, he was sent to high school at nearby Hancock Academy. Franklin did not like going to class, and he ran away from Hancock. His father sent him right back.

In 1820, when Pierce was 15, he entered Bowdoin College in Brunswick, Maine, which is shown above. At college Pierce was outgoing and popular. Instead of studying he spent a lot of time hunting, fishing, and walking in the woods with his friends. This put him at the bottom of his class at the end of his second year. Ashamed, Pierce decided to change his ways and work hard. As a result he graduated fifth in his class in 1824. Pierce then decided to study law. After three years of training under different lawyers, he became a lawyer in New Hampshire.

1

You are going to draw Bowdoin College, where Franklin Pierce went to school. Start by drawing a straight line. Add more lines to form three rectangles for some of the school's buildings.

2

Add a rectangle to the top of the building on the left. Add a triangle and a half circle to the one in the middle. Add the shape to the top of the next building. Draw the slanting shape as a guide for the buildings on the right.

3

Add straight lines inside the building on the left. Add lines inside the half circle in the middle building. Draw a small roof on the left side of the last shape. Add a square to the right side. Draw the small tree. Add squiggly lines for more trees to the left.

4

Erase extra lines. Starting at the left side of the slanted shape, draw a vertical line to meet the roof you drew in the last step. Next draw the lines for the roofs and outlines of the next two buildings. Next draw two tall tower shapes. Finish with the lines for the last two buildings.

5

Erase any extra lines of the slanted shape. Add chimneys to the buildings. Draw more trees and bushes in front of the buildings. Add the details as shown inside the two tower shapes you drew in the last step. Add a door to the building on the right. Add a roof line to the building to the left of the towers.

6

Erase any extra lines. Draw a lot of squiggly lines for the trees in front of the buildings on the right. Draw the many vertical lines for the tree trunks.

7

Erase any extra lines. Look carefully at the drawing and fill in all the windows inside the buildings. Some are rectangles, some are squares, and some have slight arches.

8

Look at the picture on the opposite page and add as much detail to your drawing of Bowdoin College as you would like. Finish with shading. Well done. You did a really super job.

Old Hickory and Young Hickory

Shortly after opening up a law office in Hillsborough, Franklin Pierce became involved in politics. His father had been elected governor of New Hampshire in 1827, and in 1828 Pierce worked to get his father reelected. That year he also spoke in front of nearly 500 people in Hillsborough in support of Andrew Jackson, who was running for president. Jackson, shown above, was a hero in the War of 1812, where he got the name "Old Hickory," because his troops thought he was as tough as a hickory tree. Jackson believed in states' rights to choose their own laws, a principle the Pierce family supported.

In 1829, Jackson became president, Benjamin Pierce began a second term as governor of New Hampshire, and Franklin Pierce was elected to the state legislature. Franklin Pierce was voted in three more times and was chosen as Speaker of the House in 1831 and 1832. During Jackson's presidency, Pierce became known as a dependable Old Hickory supporter, so much so that he earned the name "Young Hickory."

1

Start the drawing of the statue of Andrew Jackson with a rectangle. This is a guide for the rider. Next draw two ovals and a circle. These are your guides for the horse.

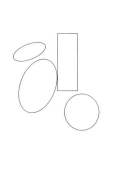

2

Use curved lines to connect the shapes to create the horse's body and neck. Add guides for the tail and legs. Use the small oval to create a detailed outline of the horse's head.

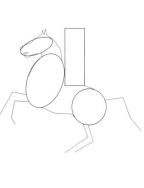

3

Erase the head oval. Draw the outlines of the horse's four legs and bushy tail. Draw the small curving line to the large oval. Add two straight lines at an angle, as a guide for the rider's leg.

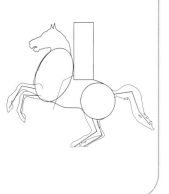

4

Erase the guidelines for the horse. Using the rectangle and the leg guide, draw the outline of the rider as best you can. See how he is raising his hat, and how his second foot is behind the first.

5

Erase the rider guides. Draw the reins, saddle, and stirrups of the horse as shown. Notice the round shapes of the reins at the horse's mouth. Next draw the sword as shown.

6

Add details as shown to the rider's hat, as well as the hand that is holding the hat. Add more details to the rider's jacket and leg. Finish this step by adding details to his face and hair.

7

Erase any extra lines. Fill in details at the horse's head, mouth, and neck. Don't forget the flower shape under its ear. Add more lines to its body, legs, and tail. The lines on the feet make its hooves.

8

You can finish by adding as much detail as you like. You can then shade your drawing. Notice where the shading is darker in some parts than in others. Good job!

Life in Congress

After four years of public service, Pierce became known as a dependable politician. In 1833, he was elected to the U.S. House of Representatives. He served as a congressman at the Capitol in Washington, D.C., for two terms in a row. During this time slavery was a big political issue. Northerners flooded Congress with requests to get rid of slavery, while southerners maintained their right to own slaves. Many lawmakers, including Pierce, believed they could do nothing about the requests because slavery was protected under the Constitution. The Senate voted to refuse the requests, while the House chose to pay no attention to them.

In 1836, Martin Van Buren was elected the eighth president of the United States, and Pierce was elected as a U.S. senator. Because Van Buren was a Democrat and Jackson's old vice president, Pierce was loyal, or faithful, to him. He campaigned for Van Buren in the 1840 presidential election, but William Henry Harrison won that race.

1

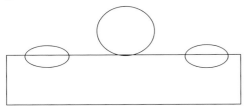

To draw the Capitol building, start with a long rectangle. Add two small ovals that cross over the top line of the rectangle. Draw a larger oval between the other two.

2

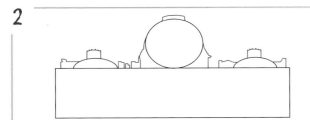

Erase the bottoms of the two smaller ovals. Beginning on the left side, start to draw the outlines of the roof shapes beside and on top of the ovals all the way across the building.

3

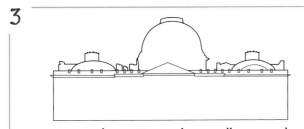

Erase extra lines. Draw the small rectangles along the top of the guide rectangle. Add a curve inside the oval on the right. Draw a triangle in the middle. Add flat, long shapes across the front.

4

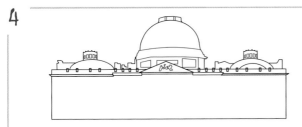

Erase extra lines. Draw windows in the roof shapes as shown. Draw small vertical lines at the top of the middle dome. Add curved lines going across the dome. Draw the shapes below the bottom curve. Add squiggly lines for the sculpture inside the triangle.

5

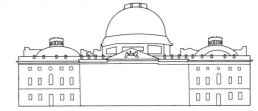

Draw horizontal lines across the top part of the building. Draw two vertical lines dividing the Capitol into three sections. Add a horizontal line to each side section, as well as squares, circles, rectangles, and arches for windows and doors.

6

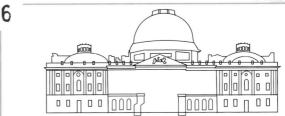

Draw columns in each side section. Add a half circle between the center columns on each side. Add the lines and shapes to the middle of the building.

7

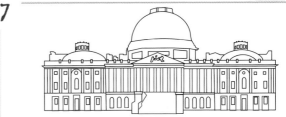

Erase any extra lines. Add more columns in the center. Draw rectangles around the lower windows on each side. Draw horizontal lines below the columns in the middle and a crooked line to show the left side of the stairs.

8

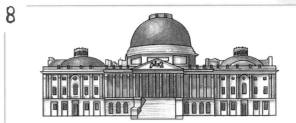

Looking carefully at the drawing and the picture on the opposite page, add as much detail to the Capitol building as you like. Finish your drawing with shading.

Family Time

In 1838, after one year as a senator, Pierce began to consider leaving Congress. He was not making much money as a public servant and he now had a family to think about. Franklin had married Jane Means Appleton on November 19, 1834. The couple set up a home in Hillsborough in 1835, but Jane sometimes joined Pierce in Washington, D.C., when Congress met. In 1836, Jane gave birth to Franklin Jr., but he died within three days. Around the same time, Pierce faced great political pressures. The strain was too much and he became sick with pleurisy. In 1838, the Pierces moved to the New Hampshire capital of Concord. There Pierce opened a new law office, shown above. Pierce took on a partner, Asa Fowler, to help him take care of business while he was away in Washington. In 1839, Jane gave birth to a second son, Frank Robert. A third son, Benjamin, came in April 1841. The birth of his sons convinced Pierce to leave public life. In 1842, he resigned, or stepped down, from the U.S. Senate.

1

You are going to draw the law office that Pierce opened in Concord. Start by drawing a rectangle. Inside the rectangle add a vertical line that is slightly right of center, making two smaller rectangles.

2

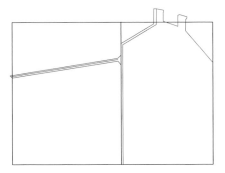

In the rectangle on the left draw three slanting lines. Add the small slanted lines at either end of the lines you just drew. In the rectangle on the right, add the line for the side of the building. Add the roof and chimney details.

3

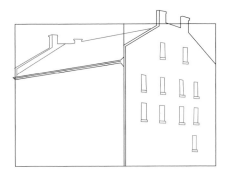

Draw the lines for the roof and chimneys in the section on the left. Notice how the roof crosses over into the rectangle on the right. Add the 11 shapes for windows to the side of the building.

4

Erase extra lines. Draw a vertical rectangle with a horizontal rectangle on top for the door at the side or the building. Draw a slanted line along the side of the building as shown. On the front of the building draw a slanted line across the top and the bottom. Draw vertical lines connecting the two lines you have just drawn.

5

Erase extra lines. Look carefully at the drawing and add the shapes for the windows, doors, steps, and signs as best you can. There are a lot of details here, so take your time.

6

Erase any extra lines. Finish your drawing with shading. Notice where some parts are darker than others. Nice job!

A Soldier at Last

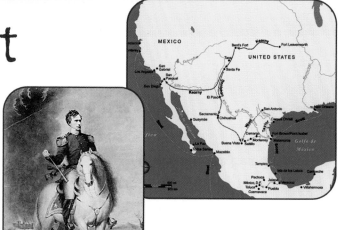

A few years after retiring from political life, Franklin Pierce finally had his chance to be a soldier just like his father. After Texas joined the Union in 1845, the United States and Mexico disagreed over the border between the two countries in the southern part of the state. The United States declared war on Mexico on May 13, 1846. The map above outlines the routes of the U.S. forces during the war with Mexico.

Pierce immediately signed up for duty and was soon promoted, or moved up, to brigadier general. On August 19, 1846, just as Pierce was leading a charge toward Mexican fire, his horse stumbled and fell on top of him, wounding his knee. He passed out, leaving his men to fight without him. The next day at the Battle of Churubusco, he twisted his already wounded knee and fainted from the pain. Despite his bad luck, Pierce did manage to fight in some battles before Mexico surrendered in September 1848, and he was praised for his leadership.

1

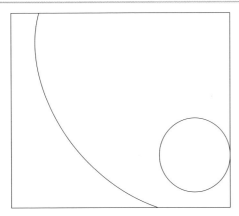

To draw the map of the United States and Mexico, begin by drawing a rectangle. Draw a long curved line inside the rectangle. Add a circle in the bottom right corner.

2

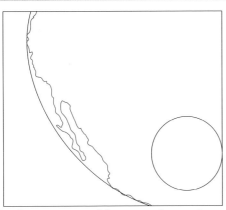

Use the large curved line guide to draw the squiggly lines that outline the western coastline. Notice the peninsula halfway down the curved guide. A peninsula is land that is surrounded by water on three sides.

3

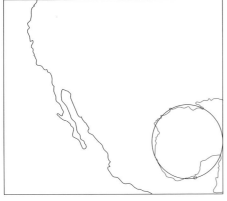

Erase the curved guide. Use the small circular guide to draw the squiggly shape as shown. This shape is the outline of the Gulf of Mexico.

4

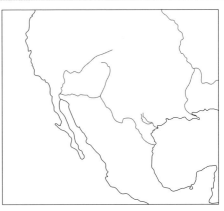

Erase the circle guide. Add squiggly lines to show some of the major rivers in the United States, such as the Colorado River and the Rio Grande.

5

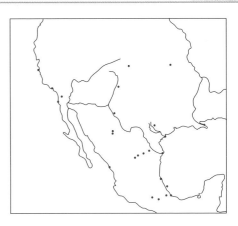

Draw the dots as shown. There are 25 in all. They show many cities and towns on the map.

6

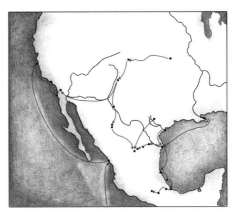

Add the lines that show the routes of the U.S. Army during the Mexican War. Finish with shading.

The Presidency

Franklin Pierce was living a quiet life in New Hampshire when he was nominated for president in 1852. Although he had not been in national politics for 10 years, he had been working as a successful lawyer and had been promoting the

Democratic Party in New Hampshire. In a meeting in June 1852, the Democrats decided that they wanted Pierce to run for president. They also nominated William R. King to run for vice president.

In November of the same year, Pierce was elected the fourteenth president of the United States. King died from a long illness a few months later, leaving Pierce to carry out his four-year term without a vice president.

As president Pierce promised to defend, or protect, the Compromise of 1850. The compromise, or agreement, admitted California as a free state, which was what Californians wanted. In defending the compromise, Pierce believed he was supporting the constitutional idea of states' rights.

1 You are going to draw the 1852 Democratic campaign poster, showing Pierce and King. Draw a rectangle. Draw one circle and four ovals inside the rectangle in the form shown.

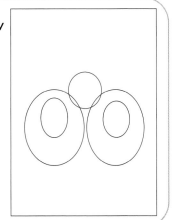

2 Draw two slanted lines that cross over the circle. Draw curved lines for U.S. flags at the ends of these lines. Under the oval shapes, draw squiggly lines for the pattern under the portraits, or pictures.

3 Erase the flagpole on the left that goes through the circle. Finish the flags. Add more lines to the circle. Add curvy lines for the flags' stripes and add stars. Draw leaf shapes around most of the large ovals.

4 Draw a triangle with a curved line on top of it. Draw lines at the bottom of the ovals and copy the candidates' names inside them. Draw the details at the bottom of the drawing as shown.

5 Erase extra lines. Add squiggly lines inside the part of the circle you did not erase. Draw the eagle inside the triangle. Add stars on both sides of the curved line. Add lines for the curtains.

6 Erase extra lines. Use the small oval guides to draw the heads of the candidates. Draw their hair and the details of their faces. Next draw the lines for their jackets and collars.

7 Erase extra lines. Add tiny lines at the sides of the flags. Draw more lines above the top sides of the portraits. Draw the pattern at the bottom of the poster. Write the words inside the ribbons.

8 Look carefully at the drawing and at the photograph on the opposite page. Add as much detail to your drawing as you like. You can finish with shading. Well done! That was a hard one to do.

Foreign Affairs

Franklin Pierce had high hopes for the United States as a world leader. As president he wanted to see the country grow in size and power. His chance to add new territory came in 1853. The Union struck a deal with Mexico to buy land both countries had argued belonged to them. The deal resulted in the Gadsden Purchase Treaty, which established what is now the southwestern border of the United States. The treaty cleared the way for the building of a southern railroad from the Atlantic Ocean to the Pacific Ocean.

Pierce also helped spread U.S. power in Asia. He allowed Matthew Perry to continue an expedition to Japan that had begun under President Millard Fillmore. Perry's job was to open up trade with Japan, which had an old rule to keep all outside countries away from its borders. In February 1854, Perry returned to Japan with navy ships and gifts such as books, guns, and model trains. The Japanese signed a treaty in March 1854, which opened the ports of Shimoda and Hakodate, shown above, to U.S. trade.

1

Now it is time to draw the ship, called a junk, as it sails into the Japanese port of Hakodate. Start by drawing a circle and an oval guide. See where they cross over.

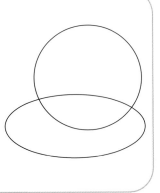

2

In the circular guide, draw a straight line and a curved line. This is the beginning of a sail. Draw a squiggly line for waves at the base of the oval guide. Add shapes on either side of the oval. These lines are part of the boat's body, or hull.

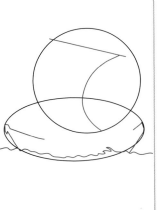

3

Erase the parts of the guides that are no longer needed. Draw the straight lines that make a mast and a rope next to the sail. This is the ship's mast. Add a square and a triangle to the hull.

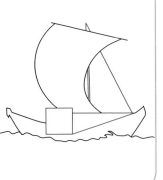

4

Draw a series of curved lines on the sail. Notice the two small straight lines at the bottom of the sail. Make sure you do not draw any curved lines inside this shape.

5

Add curved lines to the hull. Draw the line on the left side of the ship. See how this line is rough at the top. Draw a flag on the right. Add a circle with a dot in the middle inside the flag.

6

Look carefully at the drawing and add detail to the ship by drawing the rectangles, slanted lines, and curved lines around the middle and back end of the ship.

7

Erase extra lines. Add more lines and shapes to the middle section. Draw six straight lines that run from the sails to the front of the ship. See how they are slanted differently so they meet at one point.

8

You can add as much detail to the body of the ship as you like. Finish your drawing with shading. Well done! You did a super job.

A Divided Nation

During his presidency, Pierce tried to stay out of the slavery issue, believing the federal government had limited power to make such decisions for the individual states. Yet the subject kept coming up. On May 30, 1854, he signed the Kansas-Nebraska Act, believing the freedom it gave people to make choices about slavery would settle the issue. He was wrong.

Many southerners pressured Kansas settlers to vote for slavery, while northerners moved to the state to try to get Kansas to vote against it. In May 1856, an angry mob of slavery supporters set fire to Lawrence, Kansas, where many antislavery settlers lived. The burning town is shown here. To get even for the attack, antislavery men killed five slavery supporters in Pottawatomie Creek. Fighting soon broke out all over the state. The Kansas-Nebraska Act, which Pierce supported, was blamed for the hostilities. As a result Pierce lost the nomination for president in June 1856. He and his wife went to Europe, and then they retired to Concord.

1 You are now going to draw one of the burning buildings in the town of Lawrence. Start by drawing two rectangles as shown, one on top of the other. These will be your guidelines.

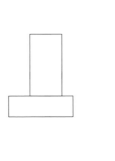

2 Draw four lines that connect to each other. Start with the small horizontal line at the bottom rectangle. Add the long slanted line as shown. Next draw the short vertical line. Finish with the long horizontal line.

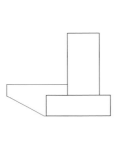

3 Using the lines you have drawn as guides, draw the squiggly line for the burning building as shown. Don't forget to add the small curved line at the top right corner of the bottom rectangle.

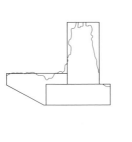

4 Erase extra lines. Add a squiggly line for the side of the building. Add more squiggly lines for the outline of the smoke.

5 Draw lines and arches for the walls of what is left of the building. Make the lines of the walls at the front slightly rough to show that the building is falling apart.

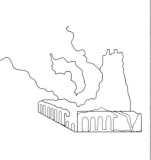

6 Erase any extra lines. Draw squiggly lines around the bottom of the building for the ashes that have fallen from the fire. Add more arched windows and lines to the tall part of the building.

7 Draw curvy lines at the side of the building for more ashes. Add lines inside and around the arches at the front of the building. Add the long squiggly line inside the tall part of the building.

8 Finish your drawing with shading. Notice that the shading is darker in some parts of the building than in others. Use light shading for the smoke, which you can rub in with your finger.

Following the Founding Fathers

In 1861, the U.S. government was at war with 11 southern states that had withdrawn from the Union. Franklin Pierce was asked to talk to northern and southern leaders to try to settle differences and avoid civil war, but he refused to get involved, or drawn in. He opposed the war, 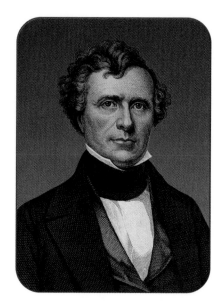 but he believed that the southern states had the right to make their own decisions about slavery, and that northerners had no business telling them what to do.

Slavery is seen as morally wrong today. Back then, however, many lawmakers, especially Pierce, believed the law was on the South's side. Pierce had no interest in slavery itself. He did not own slaves, and he did not gain anything by siding with the South.

Franklin Pierce did what he thought he could do for the United States under the Constitution. Throughout his life and his presidency, he followed what America's Founding Fathers wrote, and he stood by his beliefs, no matter how unpopular they were.

1

Begin the portrait of Franklin Pierce with a rectangular guide. Draw an oval. This will be the guide for the head. Add a vertical line.

2

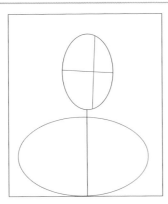

Draw two slanted lines inside the oval as guides for the face. Notice that the vertical line is off-center to the right. Draw an oval around the vertical line you drew in the last step. This will be your chest guide.

3

Draw a squiggly line for the hair. Add the shoulders and the front of the jacket using the chest oval and vertical line to guide you.

4

Add lines for the lapels of the jacket. The lapels are the long shapes at the sides. Add curved and squiggly lines for the collar details.

5

Erase the chest and the vertical guidelines. Next draw the squiggly lines to finish off the hairline. Using the face guides, draw the eyes, eyebrows, nose, mouth, chin, and side of face.

6

Erase the rest of the guides. You can add detail to the hair if you like. Finish your drawing with shading. Well done. You have finished drawing a portrait of Franklin Pierce, America's fourteenth president.

Timeline

1732 George Washington is born on February 22.

1804 Franklin Pierce is born.

1812 The United States is at war with Britain.

1824 Pierce graduates from Bowdoin College.

1829 Pierce is voted into the New Hampshire legislature and is reelected for three more terms.

1833 Pierce is elected to his first term as a U.S. congressman. He is later reelected to one more term.

1834 Pierce marries Jane Means Appleton.

1837 Pierce begins a six-year term as a U.S. senator.

1838 Franklin and Jane move to Concord, New Hampshire.

1846 The U.S. goes to war with Mexico.

1850 Under the Compromise of 1850, California enters the Union as a free state, and the Fugitive Slave Law is established.

1852 Pierce is elected president.

1853 The Gadsden Purchase Treaty is signed.

1854 The Kansas-Nebraska Act becomes law.

1856 Fighting breaks out in Kansas.

1857 Pierce leaves the White House.

1861 The Civil War begins.

1869 Pierce dies in Concord, New Hampshire.

Glossary

administration (ad-mih-nuh-STRAY-shun) A group of people in charge of something.

American Revolution (uh-MER-uh-ken reh-vuh-LOO-shun) Battles that soldiers from the colonies fought against Britain for freedom, from 1775 to 1783.

brigadier general (bri-guh-DEER JEN-rul) A military officer.

Congressman (KON-gres-min) A member of the part of the U.S. government that makes laws.

Constitution (kon-stih-TOO-shun) The basic rules by which the United States is governed.

Continental army (kon-tih-NEN-tul AR-mee) The name of the American army during the American Revolution.

foreign affairs (FOR-en uh-FAYRZ) Issues concerning outside countries.

House of Representatives (HOWS UV reh-prih-ZEN-tuh-tivs) A part of Congress, which is the lawmaking body of the U.S. government.

injuries (IN-juh-reez) Physical harm done to a person.

involved (in-VOLVD) Kept busy by something.

lawyer (LOY-er) Someone who gives advice about the law.

legislature (LEH-jis-lay-chur) A body of people that has the power to make laws.

nomination (nah-mih-NAY-shun) The suggestion that someone or something should be given an award or a position.

pleurisy (PLUR-eh-see) A swelling around the chest that causes pain and fever.

Senate (SEH-nit) A lawmaking part of the U.S. government.

surrendered (suh-REN-derd) Gave up.

tavern (TA-vurn) A place to spend the night and eat a meal.

typhoid fever (TY-foyd FEE-ver) An easily caught and often deadly sickness that is usually caused by unclean food and water.

Union (YOON-yun) The northern states that stayed loyal to the federal government during the Civil War.

volunteer (vah-lun-TEER) One who gives his time without pay.

Index

Web Sites

Due to the changing nature of Internet links, PowerKids Press has developed an online list of Web sites related to the subject of this book. This site is updated regularly. Please use this link to access the list:
www.powerkidslinks.com/kgdpusa/pierce/